# CONTENTS

# WHO'S DRIVING THE BUS?

Redefining Leadership
in a Changing
Business Environment

**GERRY MOAN**

MONDAY

Oak Tree Press
19 Rutland Street, Cork, Ireland
http://www.oaktreepress.com

A catalogue record of this book is
available from the British Library.

ISBN 1-86076-237-9

Printed in Ireland by Techman Ltd.

# DEDICATION

---

Dedicated to two born leaders,
my daughters Rachael and Gráinne.

# *1*

# ALL ABOARD!

---

There is nothing more difficult to plan,
more doubtful of success nor more dangerous to
manage than the creation of a new system.
For the initiator has the enmity of all who profit
by the preservation of the old institution
and merely lukewarm defenders in those who
would gain by the new one.

## MACHIAVELLI

It would be a truism to say that the Irish business scene has undergone seismic change over the past decade. Change has affected every aspect of our business life.

Our economy is now dominated by very different types of business from those that once characterised the Irish business scene. The management structures of these businesses are very different from the structures known to previous generations. The size and make-up of the employment pool have greatly altered. The needs of the recruitment industry and of HR management are totally new. There is also a new awareness of the importance of corporate learning and management training, which were not exactly high priorities in days gone by.

I think it would be a mistake to believe that the current downturn in the economy will slow down the pace of change. Whatever upheavals the economy goes through, I believe that the present change process will not run out of steam. Anyone banking on a slower pace of change is making a serious miscalculation.

The economy may be losing speed, but the change process is certainly not. One of the critical features of the current change momentum is that it is impossible to turn back the clock. Change has become an integral part of our business environment. The changes already instituted are here to stay. New changes are being introduced at breakneck speed. And there is every reason to believe that the pace of change will accelerate even faster as we progress further into what is proving to be a tumultuous decade.

As a management trainer closely involved with Irish business and public organisations, I have been both a spectator and a participant in the changing Irish business scene. I have experienced at first hand the dynamic period of change that has so altered the local business-scape. In the course of my corporate training work both North and the South, I have met owner managers and employees from over 1,000 small and medium enterprises (SMEs). I have also worked with dozens of major corporations and organisations.

All these encounters at the coalface of Irish enterprise have provided me with valuable insights. Not only have I had the pleasure of delivering training to so many different companies, I have also had the opportunity to talk at length with the participants in the training. Their feedback and their insights have contributed greatly to my understanding of what makes managers tick. In particular, I have always been fascinated by the subject of leadership.

During my daily exposure to so many managers and employees, I have often pondered on what constitutes a good leader. Are we born leaders or can we learn to be leaders? How much does the success of a company depend on the leadership style of the boss?

For my own professional development, I started tracking leadership performance. Over the course of time, I reached the conclusion that the dramatic changes in the corporate world have not been sufficiently mirrored by parallel changes in leadership styles. In our rush to harness the opportunities offered by the Celtic Tiger, we created, imitated and adopted a whole range of new business practice models. In the process of this evolution, we also managed to ditch many outdated management styles.

Nothing wrong with that, I hear you say. True. But I wonder whether we have replaced the old styles with adequate alternatives. Until now, I have seen little evidence to support this. On the contrary, I feel that leadership styles have failed to keep pace with the changing face of Irish business.

Why is this?

Does the fault lie with managers or with employees? Are there external factors at work here? Or could it be that the very concept of leadership does not sit comfortably with the inhabitants of this island?

To change is difficult.
Not to change is fatal.

ED ALLEN

As members of Ireland's leadership training fraternity, my colleagues and I are in the business of helping companies to develop their own management and leadership styles. If we are to fulfil our function effectively, we must hold out a vision, something for our client companies to aim for. If indeed leadership styles have not kept pace with change, we are the ones to offer a solution.

The more I thought about it, the more I was convinced that leadership styles in Ireland needed revisiting. I decided that, in order to substantiate my views, it would be necessary to conduct some objective research. I saw that a systematic and comprehensive study of leadership styles was required that would shed light on key leadership issues such as strategy development, change management, business innovation and business policy implementation.

Putting the proverbial money where the proverbial mouth is, I commissioned Amárach Consulting to conduct an in-depth research study on change and leadership. In my brief for the study, I indicated several key areas that the study should cover.

I wanted to identify what types of leadership and management styles currently operate across Ireland. I wanted to know how perspectives differed between the senior management level and the employee level. I wanted to get a handle on how senior executives and employees in indigenous Irish industry relate to strategy, change, implementation and training. I wanted to know how the consumers of leadership (in other words, employees) relate to the leadership styles of their bosses. In short, I wanted to know how managers and employees were responding to change and leadership.

I hoped that the research findings would indicate the relevance and value of various management metrics, and would provide pointers towards ways of meeting these needs.

Only the wisest and
stupidest of men never
change.

CONFUCIUS

Specifically, I wanted data that would be helpful in developing meaningful leadership training programmes. I wanted the data to suggest directions that these programmes should take. And I also wanted the data in order to challenge my own preconceptions.

In the event, the research findings have resonated strongly with my belief that there is an urgent need to revisit and redefine the issues surrounding change and leadership in the Irish economy.

I started writing this book at a time when the Irish economy was already showing signs of a slowing down. The bursting of the dotcom bubble, the foot & mouth crisis, and other macro and micro events had put the brakes on the Celtic Tiger. In fact, for several months, the very label "Celtic Tiger" was already only being used in the media in the past tense.

Just before I sent the final manuscript to the publishers, the global economy was thrown into a tailspin in the aftermath of the terrorist attacks on the American mainland. Among the many implications of these attacks, the specific targeting of the World Trade Centre meant that the global capitalist economy was now under threat.

As I write, we are only beginning to appreciate how severe the economic consequences of the attacks will be. We also have no way of assessing the fallout of any American or global response to the attacks.

If we in Ireland were only facing a downturn following a prolonged spurt of growth and boom, not everyone would see this as totally negative. Some would regard this as an opportunity for the economy to catch its breath after participating in a decade-long marathon.

But the combination of an American recession that was already threatening Ireland's business scene, together with the latest global economic nervousness, means that the Irish economy is entering a period of unprecedented turbulence and uncertainty.

This underlines even further the need for a new look at business leadership and change in Ireland. Whatever the fate of the Irish economy in the short term, I am convinced that the underlying effects of the changes that have already occurred will not disappear. At a time when the economy is struggling to find a new equilibrium, I believe that issues like leadership and management styles will become even more critical.

Along with many of my colleagues, I have long harboured the view that leadership defects tend to become less visible during the boom times. This is natural. When the economy was expanding and everyone seemed to be making pots of money, relatively low priority was given to the question of leadership. There was no place on the business agenda for such issues.

But, as the boom fades into folk memory, I believe that these leadership defects will become much more visible. We will ignore these defects at our peril. If we want to see Irish business in the hands of firm leaders, we have no real choice. We must give the highest priority to honing our critical leadership skills.

All my experience as a management trainer tells me that leadership has to be proactive. Leaders should lead. Whatever job employees are meant to be performing, they will be better off if they get their lead, their inspiration and their motivation from the top. Now, more than ever, we are going to need such leaders.

This book is based both on my own views and opinions as they have evolved over the years, and on the findings of the research carried out by Amárach. My purpose is to coherently explore how the change process has impacted on our understanding of business leadership. Ireland's business community deserves good business leaders. We need to know how Ireland is grappling with this challenge. We need to tease out the issues of leadership training for the future.

Join me as we ask: "Who's driving the bus?".

# 2

# LEADERSHIP AS A LIFE-LONG PROCESS

A leader takes people where they want to go.
A great leader takes people where they don't
necessarily want to go, but ought to be.

ROSALYNN CARTER

Leadership issues have always been a source of interest to me. I grew up in the Scouts Movement of Ireland. Much of my early thinking on leadership took place in the Scouts. Throughout my long association with the Movement that began in my childhood, I was formulating ideas about leadership. This interest in leadership stayed with me as I rose up through the ranks. Eventually, I had the opportunity to put some of my ideas into practice when I was appointed a Regional Commissioner.

One of the reasons that the Scouts made such a lasting impression on me is that the Movement itself is all about leadership. The concept was a very real one for young people looking to making their way up the ladder. I have no doubt that my Scouts training provided me with life skills that have proved very valuable in adult life. In particular, the emphasis on leadership training was to remain a constant theme as I prepared for the world of employment. Once I entered the business world, it did not take long before leadership training became my own career of choice.

I became involved in leadership training at an early stage during my years of office within the Movement. Leadership is a major pillar of the Scouts, and together with my colleagues, I was determined to play my part in turning the young people into good leaders.

We taught them that a leader should understand the needs and characteristics of each member of the group. We taught them to deal with each person as an individual, treat that individual with respect, help the person grow, and create trust and among group members. We taught the aspiring leaders to use all the resources in the group, including the human resources. We explained the difference between knowledge, which is what you learn through familiarity or experience, and skill, which is the ability to use what you know. A leader should harness both the knowledge and skills of group members to get a job done. We taught our young Scouts that the leader is responsible for developing a plan, and for showing the group achieve this plan. We showed that setting an example is probably the most important leadership skill, and that it can be even more effective than verbal communication.

When I look back at what we were trying to inculcate into these future leaders, I can now see obvious parallels with what we try today to achieve in leadership training for business managers. In the Movement, we believed that leadership development must begin during the formative years of youth. We believed that leadership development is an ongoing life-long process.

I believe that this holds true in the business world as well. Leadership development is indeed an ongoing life-long process.

In the Scouts, we defined leadership as "influencing the group to accomplish a mutually agreed-upon task while advancing the group's integrity and morale". It doesn't take a huge jump of the imagination to see the direct connection with today's corporate scene. We can readily define business leadership today as "influencing employees to accomplish a mutually agreed-upon task while advancing their integrity and morale".

The Scouts also influenced my thinking in another area that impacts greatly on leadership training. As part of the team that organised the biggest international jamboree ever held in Ireland, I met a group of enthusiastic leaders from Finland. They proudly shared with me a fascinating model of leadership that they had developed.

As part of this leadership development programme, the higher you rose in the Movement's hierarchy, the more you were expected to contribute of your experience, your knowledge and your expertise. As soon as Scouts started rising in the ranks, they were encouraged to give something back to the younger members.

It requires vision,
initiative, patience,
respect, persistence,
courage, and faith to be
a transforming leader.

STEPHEN R. COVEY

If you consistently displayed particular leadership skills, you could eventually be part of the management team. But like all posts within the Scouts, this would only be for a limited time period. Because the Movement insists on a steady flow of fresh blood into leadership positions, there are always lots of people around, both current and past members, who are not holding senior positions.

The novel thing about this model was that there was no real concept of retirement. After holding office, people did not disappear from the scene. Scouts who had moved on up and beyond the ranks retained an organic relationship with the Movement. Even former leaders were encouraged to form their own groups, and these groups continued to provide guidance and assistance to lower levels of the hierarchy.

This savvy way of recycling the expertise of the organisation back into the organisation appealed to me. I felt that it made a great deal of sense to retain and disseminate knowledge within the organisation. It was only years later, when I started working as a leadership trainer, that I recognised that the model proposed by my Finnish Scouts colleagues was actually a form of ongoing in-house mentoring. The Movement was making sure that all the accumulated knowledge of past leaders was harnessed for future generations of leaders.

I still believe that this is a model that business organisations should emulate. Both from the recipient's viewpoint and from the mentor's perspective, this model is also about continuous learning loops. Everyone ought to welcome the opportunity to receive advice and feedback from trusted counsel. We should welcome the chance to continuously learn by sharing outcomes and experiences. We should regard the building of relationships with superiors and colleagues as useful bridges for future use.

But, as yet, I see no evidence that Irish businesses are clamouring to introduce internal mentoring systems that would help retain all this know-how within the organisation.

It is not that there is no informal mentoring. At lower levels of the career ladder, it is not unusual to find people around who are prepared to give hints to others on how the system works. Informal mentors take protégés under their wing. They look out for them. They teach them the tricks of the trade that the formal structure cannot, or does not.

The problem lies in the transient nature of informal mentoring. It is natural for mentors to move on into more senior positions. But if others are not willing to step in and fill the mentoring role, a gap in knowledge is created. If potential mentors are not comfortable in occupying an informal mentor role, essential lines of communication are cut.

The traditional type of mentor is an external mentor. This kind of formal mentoring can be an essential part of leadership training. Business mentors are usually practicing executives who are willing to share their knowledge and experience with less experienced individuals. Business mentors can perform several different transitional roles: coaching, facilitating, networking and counselling.

In the coaching mode, the mentor encourages the protégé to develop his or her potential. In the facilitating mode, the mentor helps smooth the way towards some future action, setting in motion other interactions that will help the protégé pursue their goals. In the networking mode, the mentor shows the protégé how access to alternative informal and external structures can make things happen faster. In the counselling mode, the mentor acts as a sounding board and confidant who helps protegés to see the bigger picture.

Yet although the benefits of mentoring are self-evident to the mentoring community, and although mentoring is now a concept that is understood by Irish business, most people in the workplace still have no direct experience of formal mentoring. This unfamiliarity with mentoring makes it difficult for some to imagine why anyone would ever need a mentor.

A leader is one
who knows the way,
goes the way
and shows the way.

JOHN C. MAXWELL

If you ask people whether they ever had an informal mentor for whom they retain a high regard, the answer almost universally is "my first boss." Many of us recall with gratitude how our first boss took us in, looked out for us, and took a particular interest in our development. Typical comments include:

*"The best person that I ever worked for."*

But even people who have good things to say about the informal mentoring abilities of their first boss are actually giving us another message: that their positive mentoring experience was a static, once-off occurrence. They remember it because it stood out. Usually, it has not been repeated since. The goodwill seems limited to our first job. After that, we are left to sink or swim.

In the employment world, there is an understanding of the concept of informal mentoring. Employees and managers do at least have the opportunity to discuss their issues with their business colleagues and with their family partners. They can turn to someone when they feel the need.

In the world of small and medium size enterprises, however, informal mentoring barely exists at all. Not because owner-managers are not interested. The opposite is true. Many owner-managers would dearly love the opportunity for informal mentoring. They would love to turn to someone when they feel the need. They would love someone to give them advice, hints and support.

But they can't. Why? Because, in the entrepreneurial world, most entrepreneurs do not have same-level peers. Unless they are in a formal business partnership, they cannot share their concerns with colleagues. And they are not used to going for informal mentoring outside their business.

The very essence of
leadership is that you
have to have a vision.

THEODORE
HESBURGH

Their predicament is exacerbated by the fact that these same owner-managers usually have non-entrepreneur spouses or life-partners. Almost by definition, entrepreneurs believe that they cannot share their issues with the people closest to them – because their spouses and partners are almost always the product of the employment world.

The mindsets and work-experience of employee spouses and partners are shaped by their being part of the employment world. They have little understanding or appreciation of the entrepreneurial world. On the contrary, many family members resent the fact that an entrepreneur became an entrepreneur. They do not understand what drives entrepreneurs. They are often the last person to turn to for informal mentoring.

This generates feelings of frustration among many SME owner-managers. They feel that they do not have a common language with their spouses. They feel blocked off from informal mentoring systems.

It is therefore no coincidence that the SME owner-manager segment is the one sector of the business world where formal (as opposed to informal) mentoring has taken hold. These owner-managers have no access to informal mentors. Their own companies are usually not big enough for in-house mentors. Consequently, it is these SME owner-managers who are most open to the concept of external mentors.

Let us return to the Finnish example. I believe that there is a case for transposing their model to the Irish business scene. If larger companies made internal mentoring an integral part of the organisational culture, there would be less of a waste of accumulated knowledge. A company's reservoir of natural assets could be harnessed continuously for the benefit of the company.

In simplest terms,
a leader is one
who knows where
he wants to go,
and gets up, and goes.

## JOHN ERKSINE

This chapter has described how my Scouts experiences helped mould my interest and later career in leadership training and mentoring. I was introduced to the concept of continuous learning loops, which I later applied not just to career path strategy but to job satisfaction, morale and all-round motivation. I learned that every individual should be a leader in himself or herself. And I learned to value the role of leadership in driving any organisation forward.

Of the best rulers,
The people only know that they exist;
The next best they love and praise
The next they fear;
And the next they revile.
When they do not command the people's faith,
Some will lose faith in them,
And then they resort to oaths!
But of the best when their task is accomplished,
their work done,
The people all remark,
"We have done it ourselves."
Lao-Tzu, Chinese philosopher, 600 BC

# 3

# COPING WITH CHANGE VS. ATTITUDES TO CHANGE

---

Things do not change; we change.

HENRY DAVID THOREAU

Lots of different factors influence our perspectives in relation to change, leadership and strategy. In this chapter, we examine our attitudes to change, we look at how we cope with change, and we ask how our perspectives of change mirror the way we relate to the organisations that we work in.

Whether we're the boss sitting in the driver's seat, or we're an employee who has not yet reached the senior management level, it is inevitable that our perspectives will be affected by our attitude towards our company. The degree to which we like our company, think it is doing well, or consider that management is leading the company in the right direction, will colour our attitudes.

For example, if we have a problem with the whole management ethos of the company we work in, we are more likely to disapprove of the changes that have been instituted. But if we can identify with the decisions that have shaped company policy, our attitude to the changes will take on a different hue.

The prosperity and success of the company we work in also influences our attitudes. It is much easier to develop a positive attitude to a company that is flying high and that is paying us well, than to a company that is struggling and paying us badly.

Our positive or negative attitudes to change, leadership and strategy are also dictated by our view of the sector within which our business operates. If we have been working in recent years in agriculture, public services or retail banking, we will be acutely aware that our sectors have suffered from a bad press. Both within and without, these sectors have been assailed. They have consistently been accused of being fuddy-duddy, behind the times, antiquated, out of touch and resistant to modern trends.

At first people refuse to
believe that a strange
new thing can be done,
then they begin to hope
that it can be done,
then they see that
it can be done – then it
is done and all the world
wonders why it was not
done centuries ago.

FRANCES HODGSON
BURNETT

If, on the other hand, we have been working in retailing, manufacturing, some of the newer financial services, or until recently in dotcoms and telecoms, we will have developed more upbeat attitudes. These are sectors that have been experiencing many of the benefits of the boom. These are also the sectors that have been trumpeted in the media as representing the new Ireland.

Yet although attitudes to change are influenced by the sector we work in, there is a universal perception that dynamic forces are driving and changing the economy. People in all sectors share a sense that the business world is operating within a powerful ongoing momentum.

This universal acceptance of change is not limited to those who have directly benefited from change. There are whole sectors of the employment scene that feel that change has done them no favours. Yet even people for whom change has had negative implications also accept that change is a constant. These people may not actively embrace change, but they display an attitude to change that is characterised by a mature sense of realism. They might have misgivings, but they have still managed to lose most of their nostalgic longings for the way things used to be.

The real question regarding our attitudes to change is how important these attitudes are in the wider context of our business life. I suspect that our attitudes to change may prove less relevant than we think. If almost everyone, whether those who are part of a high profile, upbeat sector, or those who work in low profile downbeat sector, accepts change as inevitable and permanent, our actual attitudes to change may not prove to be terribly significant.

In the choice between
changing one's mind
and proving there's
no need to do so,
most people get busy
on the proof.

JOHN KENNETH
GALBRAITH

It seems that change has become such an integral part of the story that we are now way beyond the need to debate our attitudes to change. A look at what has happened in the Irish economy in recent times reveals the tremendous scope of the changes. Whatever cross-section of Irish companies we choose to examine, we cannot fail to notice how much actual change these companies have experienced on the ground.

For decades prior to recent times, we used to regard change as an irritating variable. Change was not particularly welcome. Change was episodic. We often wished it would go away. Almost overnight, a totally different reality has emerged. Change stopped being a temporary state, and became a major constant in the Irish economy.

Of course our attitudes to change matter. But in a sense, objective reality has overtaken this debate. Today, we all subscribe to a whole new vocabulary. We accept change, without spending too much time asking whether we're happy or sad at change. When we want to describe the new situation that has prevailed in recent years, we now readily use words like evolving, changing and focusing.

By any definition, the change that took place in the Irish economy came about at lightening speed. Change has taken root in the collective psyche within a remarkably short time. We now accept change as part and parcel of the Irish business experience.

There have been some who claim that Ireland and Irish society had to pay a price in order to keep up with the pressure of the boom economy. Most of us, however, seem ready to accept the trade-off.

Like it or loathe it, change is now a permanent resident on our shores. The benefit is that we can spend less energy asking what we feel about change, and spend more energy looking at how we cope with change. In the end, it is our ability to absorb change and to live with change that will determine how we lead change.

# 4

# The Wave of Change – From Ripples to Tidal Force

---

People underestimate their capacity
for change.

JOHN PORTER

The rapid changes in the Irish economy have affected Irish business across the board. In this chapter, we will look at what the research told us about the different ways in which these changes have impacted on different types of business. We will examine three models: traditional family businesses, entrepreneurial businesses and large companies

**Change in family businesses**
By family businesses, we refer to businesses where several members of the family are involved in the management, and we usually refer to a business that is a generation beyond the start-up stage.

It is the nature of family businesses that any change will usually be tempered by a significant degree of built-in conservatism. There is often a sense of "leave things as they are". There is a permanence that characterises family businesses. It was therefore no surprise that the research indicated that the sense of continuity in a family business often brings with it a high level of control. Family businesses tend to favour the *status quo*, because the family is the embodiment of the *status quo*.

Key positions are invariably held by family members, so that there is little or no dilution of influence or control outside the family. Indeed, one of the traditional means of retaining control among longer established family businesses is to diffuse much of the shareholding and the executive structure across the cousinhood and the extended family, including sons-in-law, daughters-in-law, brothers-in-law and sisters-in-law.

A bit like the divine right of kings in earlier centuries, family businesses have a strong belief that they posses an instinctive grasp of the business. In an environment where people feel that leadership is their right, they can be less fussy about formal reporting structures. After all, it's all in the family. In family businesses, rigorous reporting can often be the exception rather than the rule.

Change does not
necessarily assure
progress, but
progress implacably
requires change.

HENRY S.
COMMAGER

In these circumstances, change tends to be less dramatic than in other types of company. However, handling change is always going to be a major challenge for family businesses. As family businesses seek effective models for handing over executive power smoothly to the next generation, the issue of change, and how it is handled, becomes even more acute. Founders and long-time heads of the business often have a real problem handing over power, even if they have groomed the next generation precisely for this.

The research also suggested that when the second and third generations do take over, they face challenges of their own. They have to find a way of countering the natural conservative tendencies inherent in the business structure and management. They need to stay abreast of modern management thinking. They need to absorb change in order that change does not absorb them. It is thanks to these new generation family management members that more and more family businesses are now embracing a plc model and bringing in non-family professional management.

Employees of family businesses often seem to display positive attitudes to their bosses. There is evidently something about being employed by a family business that rubs off on the employees too. From the outside looking in, we are often struck by the sense of common purpose in family businesses.

> "The company I work for is a family-owned
> company so I really like working there.
> The responsibilities are shared."

People who work in family companies tend to display an above-average degree of loyalty. They can tend to identify quite readily with the company's goals and business ethos.

Many employees have warm things to say about a family-based culture.

> "It's very much a family kind of organisation. There's a lot of similarity between the people that work there, a lot of the same interest."

I think that it is too simplistic to claim that employees of family businesses are being duped. Many employees of family businesses genuinely feel part of the family. And, even if we know very well that they are not, the employees themselves seem to believe that they have secured a valuable trade-off. They know that they are more likely to receive recognition for a job well done. The research shows that employees feel that family businesses are more likely to try and retain staff when times are hard. And because the bosses in family businesses tend to stay longer in their posts, employees can expect a greater degree of job permanence.

## Change in medium size entrepreneurial businesses

It is almost axiomatic that entrepreneurial businesses are headed by individuals with a strong sense of direction and a strong sense of self. One of the dominant characteristics of many medium size entrepreneurial businesses is that they were established in the image of their visionary entrepreneur founders. These entrepreneurs were driven by an idea, a vision, an opportunity. It is this dynamic momentum driving entrepreneurial businesses that makes them more open to change.

People can't live with
change if there's not a
changeless core inside
them. The key to the
ability to change is
a changeless sense
of who you are,
what you are about
and what you value.

STEPHEN R. COVEY

The research confirmed that the owner-manager entrepreneurs who establish and run medium size entrepreneurial businesses tend to adopt a very personal management style. Many of them will have practiced their managerial skills elsewhere. While they awaited their entrepreneurial opportunity, they would have been surveying the managerial styles of their own bosses. When their moment arrives and they head up their own business or take senior positions in someone else's business, they have very firm ideas of their own on how to run a business. They can draw from their own experiences.

Together with their huge personal commitment, entrepreneurs also bring clarity of motivation and clarity of direction to their new enterprises. They are not scared of change. They try to exploit changes in the business environment. They have no problem in embracing change.

When we look at the employees of entrepreneurial companies, we can discern in the research a distinct sense of ownership that is quite similar to that felt by employees of family businesses. Many employees in entrepreneurial businesses get a buzz from the power of the idea that is driving the company's founder. These employees are more inclined to view their boss as a visionary.

Employees of entrepreneurial companies accept that there is a close link between the personality of their boss and the way the company is run. In other words, they see the management style as an extension of the boss. They share the excitement of working in a relatively new business that is constantly adapting to changes in the market.

## Change in larger companies

Of the three categories of business – traditional family businesses, entrepreneurial businesses and large companies – it is the last that has experienced the most significant degree of change.

Big business is almost unrecognisable compared to where it was just a decade ago. Takeovers, mergers and buyouts litter the scene. Some companies have gone on the acquisition trail, others have been subsumed. The spate of acquisitions has left many companies trying to get to grips with merger integration. Well-known brand names have disappeared, others have been created, and countless companies have had image make-overs. Management buyouts are a further expression of the confidence that has characterised big business in recent years.

Industry restructuring has become the order of the day. A large proportion of the working public now works in companies that were the target of takeovers or mergers. We are now used to a level of mobility and impermanence that was unheard of just a few short years ago. Many companies have forsaken the traditional markets and have energetically embraced new markets. New management teams and new management practices are commonplace

The research confirmed the accepted wisdom that so many parameters have changed. Many large companies are now part of even larger conglomerates. It is rare today to find anyone who has held the same position in the same company for more than five years. In some sectors such as financial services, most people have been in their current role for less than three years.

None of us knows what the next change is going to be, what unexpected opportunity is just around the corner, waiting a few months or a few years to change all the tenor of our lives.

KATHLEEN NORRIS

At the micro level, a host of specific changes have occupied the minds of management in large companies. Different sectors are having to cope with sector-specific problems. For example, the food sector is having to cope with the decline in confidence caused by the ravages of the BSE and foot & mouth crises. The tourism sector is having to cope with the fallout from the foot & mouth crisis and the latest threats to international travel.

An interesting finding to emerge from the research is that, unlike their entrepreneur counterparts who own their own companies, the CEOs and senior executives of major companies make a distinction between holding office and owning office. Against a background of high executive mobility, such a distinction has its own logic. These senior executives know that their occupation of their desk depends on their performance. Owning office is largely a thing of the past.

Based on what senior executives revealed in the research, they are generally very connected to, and engaged in, their organisation. Many will have moved up through the ranks, and there seems to be almost no evidence of executives parachuting into the top job. After the long haul that they have embarked on to reach their lofty positions of responsibility, these executives want to survive. To do that, they know that they have to conform to an organisational management style.

On a personal level, these senior executives are likely to have experience of management and leadership training. They are conscious of the need to lead, even if no one has defined precisely what they mean by leadership. They are also aware of the limits of their power. They are becoming increasingly conscious of the need for deliberation.

The man who views the world at 50 the same as he did at 20 has wasted 30 years of his life.

MUHAMMAD ALI

Unsurprisingly, the research showed that from the employee perspective, things look different. Employees in larger companies are conscious of the number of intervening management levels that have to be negotiated. In contrast, employees of family businesses or medium size entrepreneurial companies are usually personally acquainted with the boss. It is not unusual for them to be able to pop their head round the door of the boss in order to make a suggestion or a complaint. Such behaviour is much more unusual in large companies, especially in traditional industries. The regulated nature of the work in many large organisations can generate a feeling of too much supervision.

Structurally, the degree of change in large companies has been immense for both the senior executives and the employees.

In this chapter, we examined the rapid changes that have affected various types of business, largely through the eyes of respondents in our research. What emerges is a picture of change on a grand scale. The research findings confirm what we see around us all the time, and we can safely conclude that these changes have led to the virtual reinvention of Irish business. In later chapters, we will explore how these changes impact on our understanding of leadership, and the implications of this for leadership training.

# 5

# CHANGE MANAGEMENT VS. CHANGE COMMUNICATION

---

To change and to change for the better are
two different things.

GERMAN PROVERB

Change lies at the very core of all the parameters that make up our business world. Whether we focus on the business environment, business strategy, product development, technology or leadership, change is part of the equation.

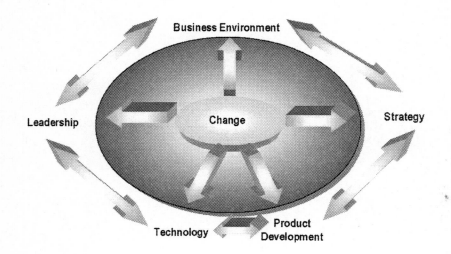

In this chapter we explore the nature of change management, drawing freely on what we learned from the research, and quoting comments made by respondents.

There is clearly a universal acceptance that change is permanent and ongoing.

*"The biggest challenge is managing change and directing it to your advantage."*

If we trace the changes that have taken place in the economy, we see that this process has been effectively underway since the 1980s. In the intervening period, many businesses have had to re-invent themselves, sometimes more than once.

*"Everyone assumes that their jobs are going
to change every year."*

It is true that family businesses are sometimes less enthusiastic about change than other kinds of business. But newer and reinvented companies have deliberately built change into the culture of the organisation.

*"The energy of the business is ever-changing,
which means that you are always changing
too."*

If we look at perceptions of change on a continuum that stretches from change as a threat to change as something wholly positive, we can identify some differences between entrepreneurs, senior management and employees.

It comes as no surprise that the champions of change are the entrepreneurs. They thrive in an atmosphere of change. They know that the wackiest ideas and the most ambitious goals have much more chance of being accepted in a fast-changing business environment.

*"You can go from being a relatively
unestablished player to being an established
player very quickly."*

Senior managers also embrace change. In both the public and private sectors, the change momentum gives them the opportunity to differentiate on the basis of improved service or product offerings.

*"It makes life so much simpler if you can be
just a bit ahead."*

A great many people
think they are
changing when they are
only rearranging their
prejudices.

WILLIAM JAMES

And even employees, who traditionally have shown resistance to change, now bow to its inevitability. Employees once occupied pride of place at the threat end of the continuum. Today, though they may not cheer enthusiastically at the prospect of change, they sit closer to the midway mark on the continuum.

*"Because change is inevitable, it's positive."*

Change does not happen in a vacuum. If change has been successfully implanted into our collective psyche, it did not happen by accident. Someone had to be managing the change process. In the work context, that someone was change managers.

What constitutes good change management?

If you ask managers, they will tell you that it must encompass a strong sense of leadership and direction. They will tell you that a good change manager has to foster a strong sense of shared understanding as to why the change was going to take place. They will tell you that change management requires a keen understanding of the human impact of change. And they will emphasise the importance of building a consensus across all levels to support the change.

Well, they would, wouldn't they?

Yet beyond the platitudes, in reality most change managers are comfortable with the process of change and with their role within it. They also recognise that in the past, change managers may not have focused enough on the people aspect. In the mad rush to handle and absorb the structural changes taking place, change managers acknowledge that they paid too little attention to the people being affected by these changes.

Change managers recognise the need to take unpopular decisions. They regard this as being part of the package of their job. Most of them do not describe taking unpopular decisions as having been a particularly painful experience. They firmly believe that there are certain decisions that they are uniquely qualified to take.

Most change managers do not feel that this makes their job more lonely or more isolated. The only exceptions to this are managers who have come up through the ranks. Such people are more likely to describe the change management experience as lonely. One of the reasons why loneliness is not a big issue for most change managers is that many derive important support and direction from members of their collegiate top team within the company.

It is easy to accept the existence of external drivers of change such as the market and the competition. We have no problem looking for new solutions within the context of these change drivers. However, there is almost universal recognition that real change can only be driven from within.

This can lead to a clash between different management groups within the bigger companies. Differences of opinion can emerge between different tiers of management, and sometimes a battle develops along that clichéd continuum - the old vs. the new.

Many smaller companies seek to foster internal drivers by deliberately pursuing a policy of appointing non-executive directors to the board. The hope here is that these often high-profile individuals will help promote change and challenge the *status quo*.

Employees have mixed views on the subject of change, ranging from very positive to quite negative. It is not the principle of change that dominates their thinking. Indeed, there is a widespread recognition of the requirement for change.

We live in a moment of history where change is so speeded up that we begin to see the present only when it is already disappearing.

R. D. LAING

For employees, the key negatives about change relate to a feeling that change is sometimes instigated on the basis of personal promotion rather than on the basis of an actual need to change.

*"Things were going well.*
*Suddenly, because one particular manager*
*wanted to do something his own way, he*
*wanted to change it. He pushed forward the*
*change, and created mayhem in the process."*

Much of the negativity surrounding change is a function of the uncertainty associated with change. When we don't know how something will impact on us, we regard it with suspicion. When we're not sure how to adapt to something new, we adopt negative feelings towards it.

Many employees identify lack of planning as an area of weakness within their companies. The change process is felt to be essentially re-active rather than pro-active. Management is seen to be engaged in fire-fighting rather than in initiating change within a well-planned agenda.

*"Companies get caught up in just dealing*
*with the day to day issues, They don't step*
*back and say okay, let's see how we can do*
*what we're doing better. They get so caught*
*up in just dealing with now that they don't*
*plan for 6 months ahead."*

The negativity associated with a feeling among employees that management haven't coped well with the change process is not restricted to the behavioural element. Just as important is managing the change in thinking.

"It's very difficult to change someone's mindset, because this sometimes means having to admit that the previous thinking was wrong. I think that sometimes it is the company that creates the mindset. There are people who have been in the company a long time. They have always worked in a certain way. Now, all of a sudden, you make decisions that effectively change their jobs. They forget that for years you've been telling them that quality is important when you're serving the customer – and now someone comes along and changes the priorities."

In terms of communications within the company, most employees share a belief that, overall, things have improved over the years. However, a large number of employees still feel that there is not enough evidence of good communication. They feel that there is still insufficient sharing of information and that there is still too little involvement in decision-making.

Based on the research findings, I believe that we can say that change communication rather than change management is the issue.

One of the most common sources of problems in manager communications is ambiguity. When managers fail to articulate their goals and expectations, employees have to make assumptions about what they are meant to accomplish and how they are meant to do it.

Any change, even
a change for the better,
is always accompanied
by drawbacks and
discomforts.

ARNOLD BENNETT

Many employees identify poor communication as a fundamental issue. Employees claim that a "them and "us" culture still pervades many companies, and this phenomenon is regarded as one of the last remaining negative aspects of Irish business.

Communicating change is clearly an area where more work needs to be done if we are to sweep away what employees call outdated management attitudes.

> "The whole thing that's changing in Irish companies recently is communication from the top of the company right the way down. The people at the bottom line need to be informed as much as the people at the top. Until the communication structure is improved, it's still going to be the Irish mentality. The managers will sit in the boardroom, while the people out on the floor are doing all the graft. The ones at the bottom get a small bonus, the ones at the top get a big bonus. The only way to have a fairly managed company is when the board communicates everything."

We can spend vast resources in ensuring that we create well-planned structural changes. Our change management structures can be great on paper. But we will lose much goodwill if the changes we wish to implement are not properly communicated. However tight the procedures we try and put in place, we will waste much unnecessary energy if the change agents on the ground feel that they have been inadequately briefed.

The research suggests that change management is well under control. The skill that still needs attention is change communication. This is what determines how efficiently change is absorbed and implemented in a company.

This conclusion has clear implications for leadership training. We need to look carefully at how we have trained our managers to handle change communication in the past, and we need to examine what to change in future leadership training programmes.

# LEADERSHIP –
# A DIRTY WORD?

A leader knows what's best to do;
a manager knows merely how best to do it.

**KEN ADELMAN**

Our experiences during the roller-coaster years prepared us well. We now accept change as a constant. No matter what sector we work in, and no matter where we are on the corporate ladder, we share a common perception of a radically changing business environment. We have grown to be more comfortable with the notion that change accompanies every aspect of our work life.

These rapid changes took place within a very tight time-frame. Any initial doubts that the boom economy couldn't last were swiftly banished. The economy showed every sign of maintaining its momentum. One is tempted to ask: Where was the famous inferiority complex that we were told had bedevilled Irish society and the Irish economy for so many years? Where were the old feelings of inadequacy that we were told had held us back?

There is no doubt that our self-image changed together with the other changes around us. The Irish workforce responded magnificently to the challenge, and there is little evidence of any lingering sense of inferiority as the Irish economy made such a quantum leap forward in such a short time.

The fact that no one feels the need to apologise for the success of the Irish economy is excellent news. Instead of wasting too much energy pondering how or why things happened the way they did, we embraced the changes with gusto. Instead of feeling the need to justify our success, we jumped at the chance to harness new opportunities. We just got on with it.

Wait a minute. Who is "we"? Who or what was the impetus behind these major changes?

Well, it depends on whom you ask. If we were to seek the opinions of outside observers – let's say international economists or foreign dignitaries – they think they know exactly where the credit lies: with the State. Foreign observers have no hesitation in telling you that it was the State that successfully nurtured the boom economy. They will point out that it was the State that initiated far-reaching and forward-looking policies in the seventies and eighties. They have no doubt that it was the State that assembled the necessary components and prepared the groundwork for what was to become known as the Celtic Tiger.

From the inside looking out, however, the view is very different. Our research showed that when you ask Irish people about the role of the State, the answers are quite surprising. They perceive the role of the State as less relevant than we might have expected.

You can test this among your own circle of friends. How many people do you know who are prepared to give successive Irish governments full credit for creating the conditions that spawned the boom economy? I doubt if there will be many.

We hear in the media those who say that there is also a positive side to this downplaying of the role of the State. My own opinion is that this is probably based on a confusion between State intervention and State initiative. The degree to which the State is responsible for the Celtic Tiger is not related to the extent to which the State intervenes in the business world. In any event, another positive aspect of this is a change of mentality regarding government grants. The former knee-jerk expectation of grants has become much less prevalent.

But let us return to the reluctance to see the State as responsible for the sea-change in the economy. We all profess to accept and embrace the changes that have transformed the economy. But if we do not regard the State as the natural driver of these changes, who else is there to thank?

Logic dictates that we should thank those who occupy the top positions in the business world. If we're not thanking the State, surely we should be thanking the CEOs, the entrepreneurs, the mavericks, for their foresight and leadership.

Wrong.

I do not believe
you can do today's job
with yesterday's
methods and
be in business tomorrow.

NELSON JACKSON

The logic doesn't seem to work here. It seems that we do not thank our business leaders for helping us get where we are today. In fact, we don't thank anyone. Thanking is not a ready part of the Irish business lexicon.

This is very different from the situation in most Western countries. There, you do indeed find that top business leaders have become household names. Their public utterances are quoted, their lifestyle is emulated, their opinions are revered. These business leaders are admired, and are often given equal or greater status than the political leaders.

The research showed us strongly that when you ask Irish employees to give examples of "a leader", you meet a wall of incomprehension. The notion of leader or leadership is not readily understood. Most people are hard-pressed to give any example at all of a leader. A few mention the names of political leaders. One or two mention the name of a British or American business leader. But only a very small minority volunteer the name of an Irish business leader.

Why are Irish business leaders so short-changed? Why is leadership such an ill-recognised currency in Ireland? And how was it possible for the Irish economy to charge ahead at such a speed if we did not have visionary leaders in the driving seat?

If the State wasn't driving the bus, and business leaders were not driving the bus, who was?

I don't think we need to look far for the answer. By any objective parameter, the State's role in laying the groundwork for the economic boom must be acknowledged. By the same token, we must acknowledge that the insight and the energy of dozens of high-powered business leaders helped drive and power Ireland's economic miracle.

So why is the role of these leaders largely unacknowledged? Why are we so reluctant to give credit where it's due?

The ultimate leader is
one who is willing to
develop people
to the point that they
eventually surpass
him or her in
knowledge and ability.

FRED A. MANSKE, JR.

At a political level, the fact that our political leaders are not identified or described as leaders says a lot about Irish society's attitude to politics. However, this aspect of our discussion is outside our present scope.

At the business level, the questions remain. The lack of immediately identifiable business icons in Irish business should be raising eyebrows.

There are several plausible explanations for this strangely Irish phenomenon. If we were being kind, we could explain away the lack of perceived leaders by pointing to the fact that people in Ireland lack a traditional business ideology. We could single out the strong presence of agrarian traditions, and explain that Irish business has no real terms of reference that it can look to for guidance and direction. We could say that because Irish business lacks a sufficiently illustrious past, people are not familiar with the *persona*.

Continuing in our benevolent mood, we could show that Irish business is simply too small to generate the activity necessary for creating icon status among our business leaders. We would back up this claim by pointing out that, no matter how successful Irish companies become, they can never get beyond small player status in major markets.

We could try another tack, too. Maybe it's because we simply lack sufficient information about the individuals who are steering major Irish companies. Maybe Irish business is being led by teams rather than by individuals. We can name the companies, we just can't name the leaders.

We could also claim that instead of bemoaning our unwillingness or inability to single out business leaders, we should be celebrating the remarkable fact that a society dominated by a civil service mentality should now have a more positive attitude to the business world in general.

No amount of study or
learning will make
a man a leader
unless he has the
natural qualities of one.

ARCHIBALD WAVELL

A possible way of changing this lack of perceived leaders is to establish a local, regional and national leadership awards forum that would promote business awareness among the general public. An awards system could help compensate for the relatively new status of Irish business, and the relative lack of awareness of the contribution of Irish business to Irish society.

In this chapter, we have discerned a problem with the very notion of leadership in Irish society. It is tempting to say simply that the Irish can't identify leaders because they're not used to doing so. This makes sense, but it also lets the Irish business community off the hook. In the next chapter, we will explore a less benevolent explanation for this phenomenon.

# 7

# BEGRUDGERY – A VERY IRISH ATTITUDE TO LEADERSHIP

_____

The worst part of success is trying to find
someone who is happy for you.
ANON

I cannot claim that I was surprised by the research findings on attitudes to leadership in Ireland. I have met these attitudes throughout my working life. In this chapter, I want to see whether a deeper examination of the Irish psyche will help clarify matters.

A debate exists on the subject of leaders and leadership: Are we born leaders, or is it only a question of learning a specific suite of leadership skills? There is a related debate on the subject of entrepreneurship: Are we born with entrepreneurial genes, or are entrepreneurial skills something we can pick up?

We do know that the employment status of our parents can be highly influential in determining whether or not we want to start our own business. The human capital of our parents as role models and practitioners of management skills is most likely to influence whether the next generation becomes entrepreneurs. There are marked differences between children raised in a home with one or both self-employed parents, and children whose parents work in corporate or civil service jobs.

A child growing up in a home with a strong entrepreneurial culture is more likely to foster an inclination to go it alone. A child growing up in a home environment suffused with corporate culture is more likely to also seek a job within an organisation.

Does the same apply to leadership? Are we more predisposed to become leaders if our parents are leaders? Do we pick up nuances and vibes at home that help push in one direction or the other?

At an individual level, I don't have enough evidence to support either thesis. But the nature vs. nurture debate is not just about whether family background is a determinant for leadership. There is a national dimension to this debate.

Leadership is the art
of getting someone else
to do something
you want done because
he wants to do it.

DWIGHT D.
EISENHOWER

In recent years, we have become accustomed to the notion that the Celtic Tiger has shaken traditional Ireland to its core. We all subscribe to the idea that Ireland has become a source of wonder throughout the global business world. Even China sent its prime minister over here to express a wish to learn from the way Ireland runs its economy. We have every reason to be proud of our recent exploits on the global business scene.

And yet we have discovered underlying negative attitudes to leadership in Irish business today. For a deeper understanding of the Irish psyche, we need a longer historical perspective. We need to look at the national and cultural background against which Irish business evolved. We need to ask what factors have shaped collective attitudes in the Irish workplace. We need to move the nature vs. nurture debate to the national level.

Some years back, I came across an excellent history of Ireland by Joseph Lee. In addition to his excellent narrative on the history of the island of Ireland, this eminent historian provides a very wide perspective of the social and cultural undercurrents that helped shape Irish society. In particular, he has some fascinating insights that pertain to our discussion on leadership in Ireland's business culture.

In his examination of the roots of Irish society, Lee claims that for centuries, Ireland suffered from economic sluggishness. It was this sluggishness that decreed so many emigrants should leave these shores. This sluggishness was also reflected in the high degree of internal immobility and the small scale of institutions in Ireland. He shows that emphasis on inheritance patterns combined with the highly rigid nature of Irish society created an atmosphere where envy, jealousy and spite were bound to be rampant.

Lee is eloquent in describing how these qualities are perceived to be central to the Irish way of life. He points out that the Irish have devised their own word to describe the resultant personality type: the begrudger.

The final test of a leader
is that he leaves behind
him in other men
the conviction and the
will to carry on.

WALTER LIPPMANN

According to Lee, a streak of begrudgery still runs through contemporary Irish society. Begrudgery it is something that we inherited from traditional Ireland. To understand its causes, we need to understand the structure of that traditional world.

The size of the cake in the Ireland of stagnation was more or less fixed. In such a stunted society, one man's gain was indeed another man's loss. It was not just perception that winners could only flourish at the expense of losers. It was close to reality. People knew that, if you wanted status, it was not enough to raise yourself. You also had to make sure that you prevented others from rising. Keeping the other fellow down was widely accepted as the most logical defence of one's own position.

Thus was born a begrudgery mentality that regarded anyone else's success with suspicion. This was true at a personal level – and it was certainly true at an institutional level. In highly regimented organisations where promotion is based on seniority alone, huge resentment built up among people with high ability who had no outlet to express this ability. In these circumstances, it was only natural to regard the success of others as the success of rivals.

There is another aspect to this. Ireland used to be a predominantly agricultural society. Industry was slow to develop. Commercial life was dominated by a shopkeeper mentality. The goal of many young people was to gain employment in the civil service. Business, especially big business, was not held in high regard. The role of business in stimulating the economy was not given prominence. Politically, generations of Irish political leaders expressed grave misgivings about a business world they barely understood.

If we superimpose this anti-business bias and the lack of business awareness on an underlying mentality of begrudgery, we can hardly be surprised that there was little scope for a tradition of business leadership to grow in Ireland.

To return to our nature vs. nurture debate, I believe that it is Irish history, Irish culture and Irish society that combine to predispose us to look suspiciously at the success of business leaders. It is in our nature to believe that a business leader can only have become successful at the expense of you and me.

One thing is clear. If we retain such feelings, we will never develop an objective appraisal of that leader's true contribution. If we retain the begrudgery mentality, we will not be comfortable with the concept of business leaders. If we remain not very good at seeing other people succeed, we will have a problem recognising anyone as a leader.

When it comes to home-grown leaders, it is clear that an objective analysis of their performance rarely comes into play. The strain of ambivalence that runs through the Irish psyche holds us back from recognising leaders, both political leaders and business leaders.

I believe that this same elemental begrudgery also makes us relish the spectacle of the mighty who have fallen. You only have to look at how the media reacts to the collapse of a business venture. Their tone is unmistakable. You can almost hear the glee – and behind that glee, the begrudgery.

In case anyone thinks that this is normal, it isn't. This pessimistic approach to leadership is not common to most other advanced Western societies. There are many small countries with a similar population to Ireland that have no such hang-ups. Business leaders in these countries are acknowledged. There is a national pride surrounding their achievements. There is a sense of gratitude that these leaders have created wealth and prestige for the country and for the economy.

The best executive is
the one who has
sense enough to pick
good men to do
what he wants done,
and self-restraint
enough to keep from
meddling with them
while they do it.

THEODORE
ROOSEVELT

Oddly enough, the only obvious exceptions to the begrudgery rule in Ireland are the rogues of the business world. Individuals who are regarded as chancers are more likely to elicit our admiration. We only have to think of the spontaneous "Fair play to him" sentiments expressed about prominent business people who have outwitted the Revenue Commissioners. Both in politics and in business, we secretly admire the gall of those who got away with it. We rarely use the same kind of wink and nod language to describe business leaders who have created thousands of jobs for Irish people.

Such subversive attitudes may have served Ireland well during the period of foreign domination, when we knew that we could not win by open defiance, and we could only achieve anything by guerilla tactics. But Ireland today, and Irish business in particular, deserves something different.

Our sense of discomfort with the notion of success also extends to a quickness to brand someone a failure. This too seems to be part of our Irish culture. We are so mesmerised by the fall that we forget the climb that preceded it. There is an unseemly rush to say "I told you so" when we are confronted with individuals falling from grace.

The picture could not be more different in the USA. There, they have a far more sympathetic attitude to people who don't make it in a particular business. It is sobering to remember that Henry Ford "failed" several times in his attempts to build an automobile company before he started the Ford Motor Company. Walt Disney lost all his money several times before Donald and Mickey came to his rescue.

In America, the whole attitude to success and failure is different. When people see business leaders face adversity, they will these leaders to display resilience. When something goes wrong, Americans don't look for someone to blame, they do something about it. Their mentality allows them to look forward, not back. Their determination helps them see beyond today's problems. They don't let setbacks keep them from trying again. Americans have a spirit of community and of rallying round in times of problems.

So you won't hear many people in America branding Ford or Disney as failures. Nor is it difficult for us in Ireland to accept that, for these two icons of American business, failure was a valuable learning experience. Yet when it comes to home-grown business leaders who stumble, we happily claim that they have received their come-uppance. It is clearly time to change this. Ireland has by now produced a sufficiently large number of business leaders for us to be able to emulate and learn from successful Irish models.

The very term business failure hides a more complex picture. What we brand as business failures may not be failures. Very few of the businesses that shut their doors actually fail, as defined by leaving unpaid obligations. Most business failures are due to more mundane factors: selling a business to new owners, retirement, going into a new business, deciding to rejoin the world of employment, and so on.

It will take time before old attitudes formulated over centuries of harsh economic realities give way to a more balanced view of business success and failure.

To conclude this chapter on begrudgery, we are left with a formidable challenge: how do we foster leadership in a business environment where leadership has a long history of negative associations? We have to change the old model of heralding a high flyer on his way up only to revile him on his way down. We should learn from the experiences of business pioneers, even if their businesses later go pear-shaped. We must unlearn the tradition of begrudgery if we are to produce leaders who inspire.

The challenge of leadership is to be strong,
but not rude;
Be kind, but not weak;
Be bold, but not bully;
Be thoughtful, but not lazy;
Be humble, but not timid;
Be proud, but not arrogant;
Have humor, but without folly.

Jim Rohn

# LEADERSHIP TRAINING – IS ANYONE INTERESTED?

---

Nothing more conclusively proves a man's
ability to lead others as what he does from
day to day to lead himself.

THOMAS WATSON

The issue of leadership has become a fixture on today's business agenda. But what exactly do we demand of our business leaders?

A company can be blessed with plenty of resources – strong finances, enviable market position, and state-of-the-art technology. But if a company lacks leadership, it can be compared to a driverless car that can only run downhill.

The very performance of a company is influenced and judged by the effectiveness of individuals in leadership positions. We expect business leaders to set the course, speed, and duration of the work-flow. We expect leaders to give guidance about where to go and how to get there.

We demand of leaders that they accept, embrace and manage change. They must be able to formulate a vision. They must be able to communicate that vision to others in the organisation, rather than leaving it locked up in the executive suite. They must be able to think and act strategically. And they must become human bulletin boards, who advertise the values that are rewarded within the organisation.

When we want to train our managers to be leaders, we need to identify what competencies, practices, and roles distinguish effective from ineffective leaders. If we are to help individuals develop a leadership style, we must be aware of the interplay between core attributes and the learned competencies developed over the course of a working career.

Anyone involved in the leadership training field is familiar with the attributes of leadership. The following check-list (or maybe we should call it a wish-list) is not exhaustive, nor is it definitive, nor are the items mutually exclusive. It is simply an attempt to map out some of the leadership values, attributes, competencies and traits that we generally believe a leader should have. No one person is usually blessed with the full quota of attributes, but we recognise that a good mix is necessary if we are to describe someone as a good leader. And although this list focuses on the attributes of top-level leadership, the attributes are also relevant at lower management levels. They include:

❖ **Charisma** – We want our leaders to be charismatic. We want to be able to identify with them. We want them to inspire confidence in their subordinates. We want to be proud of the impression that our leaders make on everyone who comes into contact with them – in the hope that we can bask in some of the reflected glory. We look to our leaders to mould the personality of the company they head. We want them to create an atmosphere that reflects their own dynamic personality.

❖ **Communicator** – We want our leaders to be master communicators. We want them to be able to effortlessly communicate their instructions, their messages and their expectations in a lucid and understandable manner. We want them to be able to communicate our ethos beyond the walls of our organisation.

❖ **Decision-maker** – We want our leaders to be able to make decisions swiftly and decisively. We don't want them to shirk their responsibility or to try and pass the buck. We want them to take a cool, clear look at the problems and challenges – and decide on appropriate action that will galvanise the rest of us. We want our leaders to tell it like it is. We want them to be brave enough to take unpopular decisions when necessary, and not to manipulate us with fancy talk.

❖ **Trustworthy** – We want our leaders to be worthy of our trust. We want them to set an example that we can emulate. We want to be able to believe in the integrity of our leaders. We need to know that they will always be mindful of our interests. We want our leaders to be honest with us. We want them to be believable.

❖ **Focus on the business** – We demand of our leaders that they give their full attention to the business. We are nervous if they are absent for too long. We worry that, if they become involved in too many other distractions, they will lose the plot. We don't necessarily demand that our leaders be hands-on, but the business must be their major priority.

❖ **Knowledge of the business** – We want our leaders to have the widest possible perspective on their business. We want them to be knowledgeable and wise. In today's knowledge era, we don't need our leaders to know everything. We need them to be able to search their organization for the knowledge they need in order to make informed decisions. We want them to be comfortable with relying on the knowledge of colleagues and employees.

❖ **Tough** – We want our leaders to show a tough stance when the situation demands. We don't look for meek or apologetic behaviour. We want them to show their mettle. We want them to be assertive and proactive. We want them to stand firm in the face of pressure.

❖ **Listening** –We need to feel that our leaders really know how to listen. We want to believe that whoever is doing the talking – colleagues and subordinates alike – our leaders will give them a courteous and attentive hearing. We need to feel that our leaders are not swayed by pettiness or prejudice, and that they are capable of accepting honest and objective feedback in the spirit they are given.

❖ **Fallible/human** – We want our leaders to show a genuine human side. We don't need them to be supermen. We need to feel that they are as prone to human weakness as the rest of us. We want to know that our leaders are more than just automatons with no emotions.

❖ **Intelligent** – We want to look up to our leaders. We want to admire the intellectual stature of our leaders. We look to our leaders to make intelligent choices, based on a wide perspective and not on narrow thinking.

There are some in the leadership training field who still cling to the idea that teaching and reinforcing these attributes is enough. According to this line of thought, once you have successfully identified these leadership attributes, all you need do is package them and pass them on to others.

I reject this approach. There is much more to leadership training than that. Of course we need to refer to the totality of these attributes, and of course we need to see that our leaders are made of the right stuff.

But, if leadership training is to become more relevant to the real concerns and challenges of today's business world, we need a more holistic approach that focuses firmly on results. We cannot expect any company to invest in leadership training for its senior personnel unless we also offer them the prospect of measurable results.

From a decision-making perspective, it is useful to distinguish between the two extremes of a continuum. At the one end, Leaders Who Do. At the other, Leaders Who Identify What Needs To Be Done And Get Others To Do It.

Not unnaturally, employees tend to prefer the Leaders Who Do style of decision-making. They know that leadership is more than just giving direction. Employees do not appreciate bosses who only direct but who do not know how to implement.

Good leaders make
people feel that they're at
the very heart of things,
not at the periphery.
Everyone feels that
he or she makes a
difference to the success
of the organization.
When that happens,
people feel centred
and that gives their
work meaning.

## WARREN BENNIS

*"My current boss relies on his team a lot more than we rely on him. We basically run the job for him as requested, and he turns up now and again and takes the rewards. Basically, he looks great to everybody else."*

Personal example rings a much stronger chord with employees. They admire personal example. It is easier to find the motivation to get something done when you feel that the boss is playing an integral part in the effort. If there is a perceived gap between decision-making and decision-implementation, that gap will often be filled with resentment.

Business leaders themselves are less emphatic in their choice between Leaders Who Do and Leaders Who Identify What Needs To Be Done And Get Others To Do It. Their choice will be based on what they feel best suits their personality. They have a more pragmatic approach, in that they simply want to be let get on with it.

Perception also plays a role here. Most leaders don't want to be seen to be separate from their teams. In reality, we will probably discover that the Leaders Who Identify category may well choose to pretend to be Leaders Who Do for the sake of public image.

Almost universally, leaders see the need to connect with the organisation's stakeholders: customers, staff and shareholders.

*"A leader needs to connect more with his own level and below. A leader cannot be led."*

There is no human
problem that could not
be solved if people would
do as I advise.

GORE VIDAL

Much space is devoted in leadership training literature to differentiating between a good leader and a good manager. Employees, however, rarely make this differentiation. For many employees, a good manager needs to be a good leader. For them, the terms are largely interchangeable.

What do employees demand of a good leader? Many of the attributes that employees rate highest are similar to the attributes that leadership training experts also rate highest. Employees tend to regard the ability of a business leader to be a good communicator as the single most important characteristic. Employees seek clarity. They dislike ambiguity. They want business leaders to communicate precisely what they want and what they expect.

Employees give high marks to business leaders as decision maker. They appreciate working under someone who can make decisions and stand by them. They also appreciate a good listener, and someone who is a good people person.

> "You have to be a reader of people – someone who is able to look at a group of personalities and get the best out of each one by knowing their strong points and weak points."

Consistency is another valued attribute, as is the ability to give credit where credit is due. A key source of frustration for employees is the perception that they do not receive credit for their ideas or suggestions.

> "It's very annoying if you come with an idea, and you find out 2 or 3 months later that the manager or director to whom you told the idea is himself taking all the credit."

It is even more frustrating when senior management hijack the glory themselves.

*"It happens an awful lot."*

Emotional intelligence, the label we give to an understanding of the motivational forces of self and others, plays a vital role in the leadership equation. People who are emotionally intelligent are more likely to be effective as leaders.

Becoming more emotionally intelligent is an experiential process, and is not something that can be gleaned from a self-help book. Any coherent business leadership programme must address the ingredients that add up to an emotionally-rounded leader.

The conclusion that I draw from this chapter is that leadership training will need a massive boost if it is to meet the needs of today's changing and challenging times.

# 9

# A Bus Needs Fuel – Motivation & Empowerment

---

Leadership is the most studied and least understood topic in all of social science.

WARREN BENNIS

In addition to advancing our understanding of where attitudes to change and leadership are at today, the research also generated information on the effects of leadership. This chapter looks at motivation and empowerment, and explores how these impact on leadership training.

Motivation acts as a powerful fuel. It gets us up in the morning. It powers our engine during the day. And the research indicated that for both entrepreneurs and career managers, one of the most critical motivators is money – or the fear of being without money.

*"I am motivated by money and success."*

Money is an obvious form of reward. But while money can prevent people becoming less motivated, it is not always very helpful in helping people to become more motivated.

Money, success and fame are not the whole story. Based on our knowledge of the hierarchy of needs, we know that once people reach a level where they are comfortable, money as a motivator loses much of its power.

We have little problem identifying the goals of success and wealth when it comes to the critical motivators that drive entrepreneurial decision-makers, both employed and self-employed. For entrepreneurs, motivation is second nature.

All the things that we recognise as the personality traits of entrepreneurs are mirrored in their motivation. Things like high energy, resourcefulness, determination and resilience. Entrepreneurs are driven by a fire in the belly that makes them believe that anything is possible. This fire in the belly is a very powerful motivator.

The entrepreneur's sense of challenge is another powerful motivator. Entrepreneurs are driven by a special sense of vision and originality of thought. It is as if entrepreneurs carried around their own kind of self-propulsion.

> "Two blades of grass where one grew
> previously."

The situation is different for decision-makers who work within organisations. The rewards in large companies tend to me more tightly defined. It is often the challenge of the job role, rather than an internal fire in the belly, that motivates organisational decision-makers.

> "I am a professional with a job to do."

When it comes to seeking an opportunity to realise your own potential, we are not just talking of entrepreneurs. Managers too find this a motivator.

> "You want to achieve what you think
> you are capable of."

It is illuminating to discover which descriptors decision-makers use when they are asked to identify their "best boss". A key attribute of best bosses is that they give their employees the opportunity to learn. Also highly rated are bosses who empower their employees, bosses who are good at delegating, and bosses who give their employees the latitude to make decisions. Bosses who are firm but fair are singled out for praise. Another key attribute is bosses who are nurturing father figures, people who look after their employees, who want to see them grow in their career and personal development.

I am certainly not
one of those who need
to be prodded.
In fact, if anything,
I am the prod.

WINSTON
CHURCHILL

You don't have to be a Sigmund Freud or a Sherlock Holmes to see that many of the characteristics attributed to best bosses bear a remarkable resemblance to the attributes that people articulated in describing their own style of management.

Bosses have a vested interest in believing that it is they who determine the company's direction and pace. Whether or not they created their own company, they want to believe that their leadership style is the lynchpin of the company's success.

Employee motivation has its own dynamics. Firstly, whenever the topic of employee motivation comes up, someone is bound to ask whether it is possible for anyone to motivate someone else – as opposed to real motivation, which can only come from within.

I don't want to get into semantics or enter into a logic debate exploring this question. I therefore suggest that we agree to define employee motivation as setting up an environment where employees can best motivate themselves.

Employees will always tell you that they are better off knowing what their manager wants of them. This is only possible if the information is communicated clearly to the employees. Employee fulfilment cannot materialise unless employees believe that they are actually making a difference. The only way for this to happen is when the manager is able to clearly communicate the organisation's goals.

For job satisfaction to translate into increased job performance, the goals of the employees must be aligned with the goals of the organisation. For organisations to achieve this, there has to be a sustained environment of employee motivation.

When it comes to examining employee motivators, the first thing to recognise is that different individuals have different motivators. We will gain better insights into motivation in the workplace if we first understand this basic fact.

Effective leadership
is putting
first things first.
Effective management
is discipline,
carrying it out.

STEPHEN R. COVEY

*"I think it very much depends on the
individual that you're dealing with.
Different things work for different people."*

Some employees tend to be wary about the very nature of motivators. Too many so-called motivation schemes have actually been a disguise for bullying.

*"There are different ways to motivate people.
I find that the wrong manager can end up
being a bully instead of being a motivator."*

Nevertheless, there are certain core motivators that are shared by many employees. Challenge, for example.

*"Give people a challenge,
give them more responsibility."*

In the wake of the boom economy, it is no surprise that quality of life has established itself increasingly high up the motivation agenda.

Recognition is another very powerful motivator for many employees. When reward for a job well done comes in the form of recognition, there is often no expectation of money.

*"Tell the person that they're doing
a fantastic job."*

*"Allow them some time off for a job well done."*

Conversely, lack of recognition, lack of appreciation and lack of proper communication can be a serious demotivator.

If recognition is not given sincerely, employees will rightly interpret this as manipulation. Without ongoing acknowledgement of success, employees can become cynical.

*"People won't work well together if they do not understand where it is that they are supposed to get to, and if they don't understand the reasons why something is necessary."*

Employees learn to decipher the signals emanating from management. A boss who is not motivated has little chance of motivating employees. A boss who is fired with enthusiasm makes it easier for others to be enthusiastic.

*"Morale is low – they can't do the job they want."*

Employees can also distinguish between concern and attention. They will often be more motivated when they feel that management is concerned for them than if they feel that management is paying too much attention to them.

One of the new buzzwords to have entered the language in the wake of the changes generated by the boom economy is employee empowerment.

Empowerment is not about giving someone open-ended responsibilities with no boundaries. In fact, empowerment is not about giving someone else anything. It is about taking on greater responsibility and accountability. Empowerment thrives best in an environment where the leader provides focus, clarity and discipline, and where creative thinking and initiative are not stifled by rigorous rules and deadlines.

We don't have to look back far to a time when people in Ireland would have laughed at the very notion of empowerment. In the bad old days of chronic unemployment, we were happy to have a job – any job. We spent relatively little energy examining whether or not we had empowerment.

The boss drives group members; the leader coaches them.
The boss depends upon authority; the leader on goodwill.
The boss inspires fear; the leader inspires enthusiasm.
The boss says "I"; the leader says "We."
The boss assigns the task; the leader sets the pace.
The boss says, "Get there on time"; the leader gets there ahead of time.
The boss fixes the blame for the breakdown; the leader fixes the breakdown.
The boss knows how it is done; the leader shows how.
The boss makes work a drudgery; the leader makes it a game.
The boss says, "Go"; the leader says, "Let's go."
Author unknown

But in an environment of full employment, we become less fearful of losing our jobs. The threat of being made redundant loses much of its intensity when you know that you will almost definitely find another job. When you are no longer scared of the consequences of making demands about your working environment, you will be more emboldened to raise contentious issues.

The Celtic Tiger was never just a description of the Irish economy. It was also a mindset shared by most of the stakeholders in the economy, a mindset that impacted hugely on the entire social as well as economic fabric of the country.

Whenever we mentioned the dynamic Irish economy, we were also referring to the confidence that drove the economy. We embraced the changes as part of our personal desire to realise our ambitions. A wellspring of innovation and confident expectations helped power us and the economy ever upwards.

We welcomed the greater element of choice that a boom economy brought in its wake. It started becoming more important to us that we were known as individuals, rather than as working for our particular employer. Today, we are more likely to state proudly "I'm an IT troubleshooter" than to use the old terminology, "I work for XYZ company".

Confidence and drive have not always been regarded as compliments. In many parts of Ireland, particularly the more rural areas, "keeping your head down" and "not raising yourself beyond your station" were part of the cultural heritage passed down from generation to generation.

Our research shows that many such attitudes have been swept away by the boom economy. Even people working in sectors that do not directly benefit from this boom have been exposed to a new business environment characterised by greater competition, bigger markets and wider horizons.

The greater sense of empowerment and autonomy found in large sectors of the working public will prevail, even though the boom is coming to an end.

Leaders must be close
enough to relate to
others, but far enough
ahead to motivate them.

JOHN MAXWELL

Another indication of the new-found confidence of Irish managers is that they express relatively little fear with regard to how they would be described as managers by their superiors, colleagues and employees.

There is also another side of the coin. The competitive nature of the workplace also led to a perceived loss of personal control in certain sectors. In large companies, the hospitality industry, healthcare, agribusiness, food and IT manufacturing, the realities of the marketplace often led to tighter managerial policies. It is only entrepreneurial businesses and smaller SMEs where there is a perception of greater control.

Empowerment is expressed in many different ways. We see it in the greater confidence displayed by people in the workplace. We see it as people declare their growing belief in the art of the impossible. We see it in the swelling numbers enjoying ever-wider access to sources of knowledge.

> "It's nicer working in Dublin now than it
> would have been five years ago because there's
> a lot more for the employees."

I have heard people question whether employee empowerment is in fact an objective part of the work scene. Some ask whether employee empowerment is just a myth that management invented and that employees cling to. Others claim that employee empowerment comes at the price of weakened managerial responsibility.

We also hear that the shift from an individual responsibility culture to a sharing culture has created an environment where no-one is ever to blame. If employee empowerment is taken to an extreme, we are told, there is a danger that the sharing culture will cause us to dumb down.

In terms of management, these questions may turn out to be superfluous.

A boss is interested in
himself or herself,
a leader is interested in
the group.

RUSSELL H. EWING

Whether employee empowerment is based more on perception than on reality, the bottom line is that thousands of employees out there believe that they have a greater degree of empowerment.

> "The culture has moved from being one of individual responsibility to sharing."

In management training terms, the real issue is whether bosses have the tools to handle employee empowerment. If training organisations don't help managers absorb employee empowerment into their leadership styles, they may be missing a vital ingredient of leadership training.

The research suggests an interesting corollary to employee empowerment, and that is senior executive empowerment. When you talk to managers about their own management style, many are quick to assert that their particular management style was not typical of the organisational style. The larger the organisation, the more important it seems for managers to espouse this view. Managers have a clear need to articulate their power as an individual, and to downplay their power as part of the organisation.

In this chapter, we looked at how motivation and empowerment impact on employees. Not every good motivator is necessarily a good leader, but a good leader must be a good motivator. Leadership training programme must address how a leader motivates, as well as how employees like to be motivated.

Similarly, a manager's personal style and organisational style are often closely linked. But in terms of empowerment, in terms of their need to be seen to be individual, it is hard to get managers to overtly acknowledge this. This too must be addressed by leadership training.

# 10

## SIMILAR CHALLENGES, DIFFERENT REMEDIES

---

*The genius of a good leader is to leave behind him a situation which common sense, without the grace of genius, can deal with successfully.*
**WALTER LIPPMANN**

This chapter looks at other findings from the research that impact on leadership and leadership training.

**Strategy Development**

Ireland is still trying to absorb the changes brought about by the boom. Irish business is currently trying to steady itself for the effects of the downturn.

Yet the research tells us that people across a wide range of industries tend to identify a similar range of challenges ahead. The difference lies in the emphasis.

One of the challenges is strategy management. Management needs to keep the workforce constantly informed, and a strategy management meeting is an ideal vehicle to achieve this. Strategy management can be like a rudder that keeps the organisation on course, clarifies the vision and initiates action.

Most leaders, according to the research, would like to believe that their company has a strong strategic vision. They reinforce this belief by pointing to the fact that their companies have strategy development processes in place. These processes are generally a rolling programme, with a strategic time-frame of about two years. More often than not, the same people involved in this process are usually also involved in the business planning process.

In many companies, the formulation of the company's strategic vision is usually the preserve of the top management team. These individuals jealously guard their territory. They show little desire to democratise involvement in the strategy development area. Nor do they usually involve outsiders in the process.

Most strategy development processes involve strong elements of monitoring and implementation review. Budgets are checked and formal interim reports are written. At the end of the process, a document is produced that sets out the company's strategic development programme. The company pats itself on the back for delivering the goods.

*"I don't think any organisation can get by without a strategy."*

This idealised description, however, is often far from the reality on the ground. In many companies, the commitment to strategy development remains at the wishful thinking level. Not enough time is allocated to the process, and strategic development can often be mere lip service. And even when companies do devote time to strategy development, they rarely stick to a common strategy formulation model.

If strategy development is to be effective, it must also be proactive. When strategy development is based on reaction and response, it shows. Without a bold statement of future strategy, there can be no strategy development.

*"Strategy means someone sitting at the tiller making sure that we are in the right direction. Strategy is not someone planning things we must stick to rigidly because we are responding to market changes."*

Sometimes the strategy development document itself becomes the main issue. When this happens, to the detriment of the strategy development vision, the process is in trouble.

*"I am less comfortable in a scenario where people sit down and articulate strategy, get it all written down, and get all the t's crossed and the i's dotted."*

If we don't change,
we don't grow.
If we don't grow,
we aren't really living.

GAIL SHEEHY

Another characteristic of the way many companies conduct their strategy development process is the absence of outsiders. When everything is done in-house, the strategists can end up recycling old ideas. Without external influence and input, there are limits to the issues addressed and the strategic options considered.

When challenged to explain why more outsiders are not brought into the loop, many companies will tell you that outside consultants have a poor reputation. With the exception of managers in the tourism sector, it seems that many top management teams are wary of consultants.

Does this mean that I and my consultant colleagues across the land should take fright at this finding? Should we start looking at the possibility of retraining and finding another field of enterprise?

I think not.

But this should be a wake-up call. If management feels that consultants are a waste of time, then something is not right in the way the consultant's role, function and value are being communicated.

## Recruitment and Retention

When you ask managers about the advantages of joining their organisation, their response is usually built around the soft skills. They will talk about the good teamwork that has been built-up in the company. They will describe their company as a successful story. They will point to the interesting nature of the work and to the strength of the team. They will extol the convenience and physical comforts of the workplace, and will probably try and prove that their workplace is particularly friendly to the environment as well.

We know that, at the height of the boom, recruitment and retention were a major concern in Irish business. Demand for staff in a rapidly expanding economy was outstripping the resources of the employment pool.

Recruitment agencies popped up on every corner. There was talk of importing a quarter of a million staff from abroad.

With the economy slowing down, it seems increasingly likely that unemployment will once more become a factor in the Irish employment scene. This will redefine the recruitment scene. I believe that there is a danger that the efforts that once went into staff retention will be relaxed, as companies no longer have to cope with the urgent need to find ways of preventing staff from leaving. This would be a retrograde step.

**How companies are viewed**
The research shows that managers in large companies have a somewhat ambivalent attitude to their organisations. There seems to be little consistency. Managers claim that they do not regard their companies as a machine, as an organism. They prefer to see themselves as leaders of their teams. Some believe that they involve their staff, others downplay this element. However, if you probe deeper, there is no common understanding of some of the terms of reference.

Many managers tend to highlight the role of their organisations in the community.

*"We tend to be more considerate about people and their personal lives."*

An extra perspective is available from Irish people who had previously worked abroad. The way they see the Irish workplace is often quite different to the views expressed by people who have always worked here. The returnees find the Irish workplace more relaxed and more informal. They find the workplace as more people focused, and built more around relationships.

*"It's not that we were inefficient, but we had the opportunity to be more efficient."*

The view from the employee side of the coin is somewhat different. While employees agree that organisations are more team-oriented, they still believe that the individual boss carries considerable weight in determining what happens. Employees acknowledge that their power has increased. Increasingly, they are expressing concern that this situation will change in the coming months as the stability of the employment sector is weakened.

Most employees express positive sentiments about where they work. The nature of the work itself does not figure very highly as a factor that determines whether they stay or leave the organisation. It is the people and personalities within the organisation that are the key factor.

*"The key difficulty is that guys in key positions don't have the bottle."*

Employees are as enthusiastic about good leadership as management. The fact that they make little or no distinction between the role of the manager and the role of the leader does not affect the importance they ascribe to the leader's role.

## Investment in Human Capital

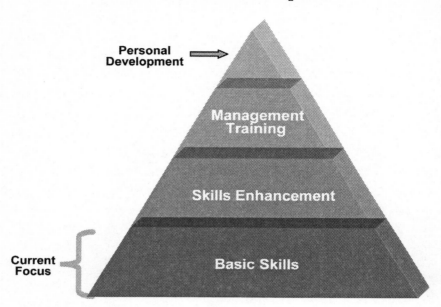

When we look at investment in human capital, we can identify four different levels in the development pyramid.

- ❖ The lowest level contains the **basic skills** that every employee needs to master any job.
- ❖ The next level up is **skills enhancement**, where an attempt is made to provide a more advanced level of competence.
- ❖ The next level up is **management training**, where suitable employees are prepared for taking on management positions, and where managers are encouraged to enhance their management skills.
- ❖ The top level of the pyramid consists of **personal development**.

We are chameleons,
and our partialities and
prejudices change place
with an easy and
blessed facility, and we
are soon wonted to the
change and happy in it.

MARK TWAIN

At present, the preoccupation of those responsible for investment in human capital is focused mainly on the lowest and broadest level – basic skills.

If we are to improve the overall quality of our human quality, we must change our focus. At the basic skills level, change will be internally directed. But the main focus in the future will be on the next two levels up the pyramid.

Skills enhancement will involve internally-directed change, while management training will involve both internally and externally-directed change. Further down the line, the focus will move up again to personal development, which will involve externally directed change.

## Investment in Human Resources

The research findings suggest that the extent to which a company invests in human resources can often be a function of the scale of the company. Smaller companies are extremely task and skill training focused. Many of these companies can regard investment in HR as a luxury that they cannot afford.

With the more traditional companies, the attitude is even more extreme. Many of these companies still see investment of this kind as no better than a necessary evil.

Newer employees in more modern companies have been exposed to a business environment where there is a wider acceptance of HR investment. These employees now expect it. Employees with no experience of the more modern way of doing things still resent it.

By definition, the benefits of task-based training are easier to measure and easier to demonstrate. In larger companies that are undergoing rapid change, there is often a preference for on-the-job training.

By and large, it is clear that many companies do not yet fully understand the need for personal development programmes, and do not appreciate the benefits that these can bring.

In the area of HR investment in leaders, most companies adopt an unstructured approach.

Performance monitoring, on the other hand, is widely adopted. Some organisations assign a critical role to team peer assessment. In most companies, it seems that the degree of HR investment is down to individuals driving their own agenda where necessary.

When we look at the overall training and development spend, a rather grim picture emerges. The spend is low by any standards, usually in the range of €127 to €1,270 per person per annum. One exception is merger situations, where companies have to invest in order to create consistency of knowledge and competence across the newly merged entity.

> *"You've got to analyse where a person's starting-off point is. Different people in the same room can be at different levels."*

Those companies that operate training and personal development programmes identify the ability to tailor the programmes to the individual's need as a key measure of success. Another critical factor in how successful these programmes are is the quality of the presenter.

> *"It was brilliant because they spent a lot of time checking out what your needs were. They kind of made the course to suit you."*

**Training and Personal Development**
In order to obtain some valuable feedback on the training needs of a company, it is instructive to speak to employees. When asked to identify the key development programmes suitable for the decision-makers in their organisation, they have very definite ideas.

Communication and self-awareness programmes are themes that are repeated again and again. Employees know a good communicator when they are managed by one – and they can spot a poor communicator a mile off.

> *"I would send my manager for communication training. He has very good vision, but he's not very good at communicating the vision back to the staff."*

Employees also want to see their decision-maker bosses learn how to listen. They want bosses to show a degree of humility, and not assume that they have all the answers.

*"I would send my boss on the 'I'm not always right' course."*

Employees want to be treated with respect. It's easy for anyone to stand up and say, "I am a people person". But in their dealings with their employees, they often fail to display these skills.

*"My boss needs to attend a people skills course."*

It is clear from the issues explored in this chapter that the "customers" of leadership have their own ideas about what leadership means. The implications for leadership training are clear. If we are to train new breed of business leaders, we have to make them much more aware of how their employees view their actions, their policies and their behaviour.

*A boss creates fear; a leader confidence.*
*A boss fixes blame; a leader corrects mistakes.*
*A boss knows all; a leader asks questions.*
*A boss makes work drudgery; a leader makes it interesting.*
*Anon*

# 11

# CAREER PATH - HARD OR SOFT LANDING?

---

You must be the change
you wish to see in the world.

MAHATMA GANDHI

In earlier chapters, we looked at how underlying factors within Irish society influence our attitudes to leadership. A remark by one of the respondents in the research, to the effect that our career paths are less chosen than determined, has particular relevance to the way we view the concept of employment in Ireland.

In this chapter, I want to ask whether we are doing a good job in preparing our youngsters for the world of employment. I want to explore whether we could be doing things differently, and whether the way we educate our children influences attitudes to leadership. And naturally, we will ask how this impacts on leadership training.

I suggest that many of us start our work career in a state of some confusion. Even prior to the boom times, when there was high unemployment, the career chosen was less than deliberate for those of us who decided to stay and work in Ireland. There wasn't a huge amount of choice. And today, with (at the time of writing) full employment, our career paths still owe more to chance than to planning.

Objectively, any observer would say that we do plan our careers. We are programmed at school to reach certain levels of competence, and we fill the places in the workplace. But in the process, confusion still reigns.

During our school days, we are urged to do well and strive to gain qualifications. When we enquire why we need to study, our parents, our teachers and society at large all sing from the same hymn sheet: "You study in order to get a good job".

Society needs us to join the job-market. Our education progresses against the backdrop of this expectation. We are actually being geared for the workforce, and most of us oblige with no questions asked. We subscribe to the holy grail of employment. Our sights are set on landing the good job our parents wished for us. We want a job with security. A job with a good pension.

But during our school career, we are not given a very clear idea of what having a job means. When we enter the job-market, clutching our qualifications in our hands, we often experience a rude awakening. To our surprise, we discover that the job-market is a much vaguer concept than we were led to believe.

We discover that the ideal of "job for life" has all but disappeared. In fact, we discover that the very definition of "job" is rapidly changing. The stability that we expected proves to be ephemeral.

Newcomers entering the job-market discover an ever-changing environment. Companies are increasingly unbundling and farming out activities. Laptops, cell phones and the Internet are increasingly helping to make central offices redundant.

People who choose the entrepreneurial route can sometimes travel an easier path. They know deep down that they want to work for themselves. Their determination to set up on their own eventually helps carry them through a series of jobs that only reinforce their vow to stop working for someone else as soon as possible.

For people who enter the world of employment, and have no ambition to become their own boss, the situation can be more confused. We drift in and out of jobs, because we haven't formulated what we want out of work. One consequence of this vagueness is that we only really start thinking what we want to be when we grow up after we have already spent years in the employment world. We only start examining our own ambitions, our own needs, after we have already blindly followed the route taken by everyone else.

It has to be said that, despite the haphazard and erratic induction, most of us prove to be very resilient. We adapt remarkably well to an environment that is very different from what our parents experienced.

Yet I cannot help thinking that there ought to be a more efficient way for society to prepare us for our entry into the job-market. I also fear that the full employment that we have enjoyed for several years may have covered up the confusion. Trial and error works, but could we do better?

I believe that if we are to streamline career paths and help youngsters enjoy a soft landing, we must focus more attention on the interface between school/college and the workplace.

I have never felt that our school system is sufficiently geared towards helping young people realise their full potential. Even the admirable entrepreneurship schemes that some schools have adopted do not define their mission as helping young people develop positive concepts of self-esteem. In many schools, it is only during retreats and other non-curriculum activities that anyone asks children what they are about. In our rush to educate them and fill them with information of questionable value, we ignore the basics. Surely, it is at school that we should be planting a seed in children who then grow it themselves.

The secondary education system is obsessed with performance as measured by formal examinations. There is precious little space in such a system for introducing future employees into the real world of work.

The situation does not always improve as school leavers become college students. Many graduates manage to complete their first degree with little or no idea of how the corporate world operates.

I see a parallel between the confusion that characterises the way we choose our career, and the confusion that characterises our later work experience. This is not to say that every career is destined for a hard landing. But much more work needs to be done at school to ensure that future adults are better equipped to enter the real world of employment.

If we are serious about leadership training, we can't afford to wait until future leaders enter the job market. If we want people to start their working careers with more understanding and knowledge, we must expose them earlier in their lives to the world of employment, the world of business.

And that means that we must start the process at school. We need to develop more models of school-business partnership. Business should sponsor entrepreneurial initiatives. It is too important to leave this in the province of government.

If younger generations enter the workplace with a keener appreciation of the world of employment, there will be less basic training to do. If we can provide a softer landing, we will be able to raise the overall level of training, and we will be able to spot our potential leaders earlier.

# 12

# Towards a Better Understanding of Leadership Training

---

*You manage things; you lead people.*

**REAR ADMIRAL
GRACE MURRAY HOPPER**

Plato argued that it takes 50 years to train a good leader. Most companies do not have that sort of time-frame to spare.

At the opposite end of the time/investment spectrum is the quick-fix leadership training programme. Most companies will not find this to be an adequate response to their needs.

I believe that leadership training should combine both ends of the spectrum: something that produces the results of a Plato-style life-long programme, within a time-frame that most companies can live with.

This book was prompted by a wish to explore more deeply who is driving the bus of Irish business. To do so, I initiated research on the current state of change and leadership awareness in Ireland. The findings confirm the need to redefine these issues if leadership development is to become the integrated, ongoing long-term process that Irish business needs. As the economy struggles to find a new equilibrium, leadership and management styles will become even more critical.

This concluding chapter summarises some of the issues to be addressed, and suggests a number of guidelines that I believe should shape the future development of leadership training in Ireland.

Change lies at the heart of the challenge facing businesses and management today. The changes in the economy in recent years have led to the virtual reinvention of Irish business. Our ability to absorb change and to live with change will determine how effectively we lead change. The role of the leader within the company is fundamental in identifying and managing change decisions. The leader is the key strategy-maker who shapes the culture within the company. Communicating change must be a key component of any programme developed to enhance either personal or management effectiveness. If we are to successfully implant change into our collective psyche, we need our leaders to be change-managers. They must give direction, and they must foster a shared understanding as to why the change was going to take place. We must give more attention to the people being affected by these changes, and we must appreciate the human impact of change.

One-shot programmes cannot miraculously transform managers into leaders. These programmes can help create an awareness of what leadership is, but effective leadership training needs to involve a mix of initiatives that occur over a longer time frame. Too many leadership programmes have a shelf-life of a few days or weeks after the sessions end. We need to develop more programmes that have effective transfer mechanisms to bring leadership skills directly back to the reality of the workplace. We need a multi-tiered approach with a single-minded focus on results. Otherwise, we may well have wasted precious time and energy.

Leadership programmes must be more than attending a one-hour pep talk with a motivational speaker. It is all very well emerging all fired up, ready to rush back to the office to give vent to all that motivation that has been kindled in us. But unless we are also given implementation tools, the enthusiasm wears off, and the effectiveness wanes. We also have to be sure that the workplace is ready to welcome our new leadership understanding. Unless our workplace provides us with fertile ground for encouraging vision, there is nowhere to transfer our new stores of emotional fuel.

Companies must do more than simply express interest in and support for the leadership programmes that they are implementing. They must make a genuine commitment to the successful realisation of the leadership training. If the CEO is not personally committed, there is little hope of it succeeding. Senior management must also walk the talk. Senior management has to be prepared to practice visibly the techniques being taught in the classroom and to make investments that affirm their commitment. Companies that do the best job at creating leaders are based on a culture that values and rewards leadership. And to achieve best results, as many of the management team as possible should be involved in leadership training, since this will ensure a shared mindset throughout the company about what leadership really is.

We need to ask how teachable are leadership skills. Some skills like communications skills can often be relatively straightforward and teachable. It's trickier when we try to teach vision skills. In addition to vision building exercises, we also need to give advice on choosing work experiences that facilitate future vision.

Business leadership must be more than developing outgoing, well-liked and charismatic individuals. Business leadership must be more than the ability to harness and synchronise the efforts of employees, or to expand their personal capacities. Business leaders also have to deliver. They have to know what needs to be done, and they have to know how to link the actions and decisions of their staff to make sure that they achieve results.

Leadership training must give added weight to the area of strategic planning. If leaders are to handle the change process pro-actively and not re-actively, we must train them to forego fire-fighting in favour of initiating change within a well-planned agenda. Leadership training needs to help companies escape from their wishful thinking attitude to strategy development. Companies must allocate more time and energy to strategy development, and must adopt a common strategy formulation model.

We must train our leaders to share information across their organisations. And that means more communication. There is little point in creating well-planned structural changes, if the changes we wish to implement are not properly communicated. We must train our managers to handle change communication.

Effective leadership is
not about making
speeches or being liked;
leadership is defined by
results not attributes.

PETER DRUCKER

We must foster leadership in a business environment where leadership has a long history of negative associations. We must address the lack of a business ideology and a lack of business leaders with whom Irish businesses can readily identify. We should examine the establishment of a forum that will examine the issue of leadership in the Irish context, and will identify appropriate behaviours. We should also consider the creation of high-profile business leadership awards, as a means to promoting awareness of the role of Irish business leaders in driving and powering Ireland's economic miracle.

We must address the begrudgery that still pervades Irish society and Irish business. In a society with a legacy of envy, jealousy and spite, we have to help transform a win-lose mentality to a win-win mentality. We must show that it is no longer appropriate to retain the feeling that a business leader can only have become successful at the expense of you and me. We have to promote a business climate where business failure is something we learn from rather than something to be ashamed of.

We should re-examine the whole area of the school-business relationship. It is at school where we should plant business and business leadership seeds in children. If we want business leadership to be a priority in society, we can't wait until future leaders enter the job-market. We need to develop more models of partnership between schools and the business community. If we can raise awareness in schools, we will be able to spot our potential leaders earlier.

There is need for greater focus on personal development across senior management. This need is driven both by employee feedback, and also by the demonstrated lack of self-awareness of senior management. However, we need to beware of an exaggerated emphasis on personal growth programmes. These programmes can sometimes improve participants' personal lives without making a demonstrable impression on their work lives.

Outstanding leaders
go out of their way to
boost the self-esteem
of their personnel.
If people believe in
themselves,
it's amazing what
they can accomplish.

SAM WALTON

Leadership training should incorporate a greater element of informal and formal mentoring. Unless more potential mentors within an organisation step in and fill the mentoring role, there will be a gap in the company's knowledge-base. Larger companies should be encouraged to make internal mentoring an integral part of the organisational culture.

We must address the less than sparkling reputation that outside consultants sometimes enjoy. There is a perception out there that top management teams are wary of consultants. We must do more to ensure that the consultant's role, function and value are being communicated.

It is no secret that many companies are reluctant to make sizeable investments in leadership training without some proof of the outcomes. There is no easy answer to this. In the short term, it can be difficult to quantify the outcomes. Patience is required. There are no magic solutions in leadership development.

If leadership training is to become more relevant to the challenges of today's business world, we need a more holistic approach. If leadership trainers are to fulfil their function of helping companies to develop their own management and leadership styles, they must hold out a vision of effective leadership. That vision must include results in the equation.

I remain convinced that the best way forward is to create programmes that link leadership training with demonstrable results. We cannot expect any company to invest in leadership training for its senior personnel unless we also offer the prospect of measurable results. And we should always be mindful that training is only one of several critical elements that create the experiences and rewards needed to develop effective leadership.

Our understanding of leadership has evolved. We now see our leaders as change-masters. We must focus on teaching managers and executives to embrace and mobilise the changes on the business horizon.

We opened this concluding chapter with Plato. He insisted that he needed 50 years to develop a leader. But Plato is not the only example in town.

Take Aristotle, for example. He claimed that he could develop a leader in 2 years.

His pupil was Alexander the Great.

# ABOUT THE AUTHOR

Gerry Moan is one of the most inspirational trainers in the Irish corporate education market.

His first experience of leadership training was in the Scouts Movement, when he served as Ireland's youngest ever Regional Commissioner. After graduating in architecture, he worked in the emerging field of geographical information systems software. Gerry entered the area of training in 1993, and became a founding partner of Optimum Results in 1995. Over the next 5 years, Gerry delivered training to over 1,000 Irish SMEs in the fields of marketing planning, strategic planning, team-based change, retail training and sales training.

He earned his Advanced Certificate in Business Counselling from the University of Durham, and is closely associated with the Durham Business School Foundation for Small and Medium Enterprise Development. He is a member of the Institute of

Business Advisors, and a former Regional Chairman of the Marketing Institute.

He has served as consultant to a number of regional and national organisations in Ireland, helping County Enterprise Boards, FÁS, Employment Partnerships and others to define and develop their own training infrastructures. He also serves on the boards of several companies involved in adapting new technologies to the SME training area.

Gerry launched Business Action Ltd. as a vehicle for delivering meaningful and measurable training to the Irish SME market.

**Gerry can be contacted at <u>gerry@businessaction.ie</u> or + 353 42 938 9999.**

Also available from
## OAK TREE PRESS

**Five Plateaus of Progress:
Practical Lessons in Self-development,
Personal Leadership and Positive Living**
Gerry Madigan
£16.95 pb : ISBN 1-86076-145-3

**Five Plateaus to Progress** provides a roadmap to
guide you through your business and personal life,
stepping up from achievement to achievement,
bringing you closer to your goals.
Each of the five plateaus — awareness, vision, discipline, change and
commitment — is part of a continuous cycle of self-development. With
inspiring stories of people who have lived these principles, this book will
help you reach new levels of success in all areas of your life.

**Agents of Change:
The Manager's Guide to Planning and
Leading Change Projects**
Pauline Hall & Hilary Maher
£16.95 pb : ISBN 1-86076-090-2

Change is the new constant. **Agents of Change**
provides the essential tools, techniques and
approaches to help managers and consultants to
implement change in the workplace.
Packed with real-life examples from Irish companies, it is an indispensable
guide for planning and implementing change projects successfully.

**Learning Skills for Managers:**
**Practical Tools and Techniques to**
**Turbo-charge Your Career**
Samuel A Malone
£14.95 pb : ISBN 1-86076-170-4

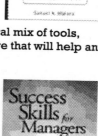

In today's competitive business world, many managers
find they must learn new skills and upgrade their old
ones through training, self-study and sometimes a
return to formal education. **Learning Skills for**
**Managers** is a highly readable, entertaining and practical mix of tools,
techniques, models, learning maps, mnemonics and more that will help any
manager learn new skills with confidence.

**Success Skills for Managers**
Samuel A Malone
£18.95 pb : ISBN 1-86076-139-9

**Success Skills for Managers** blends practical tips,
checklists, mind maps, acronyms, mnemonics and
success stories designed to help managers work
better and learn more quickly. The book offers a
model of personal and business excellence that is a
synthesis of the best available information on success drawn from
psychology, NLP, learning principles and contemporary business thinking.

**Will the Real Leader Please Stand Up?**
**A Practical Guide to Being a Manager Others**
**Will Want to Follow**
Mark Starmer
£19.95 pb : ISBN 1-86076-107-0

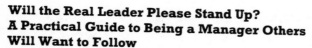

This unique book, packed with techniques, examples
and helpful suggestions on how to become an effective
leader, gives you the opportunity to obtain a free
personal profile to show where your strengths and opportunities as a leader
lie. With a host of practical advice that can be put into practice immediately,
this book will help you to become a leader others will want to follow.

Available from good bookshops, or
**OAK TREE PRESS**
19 Rutland Street, Cork
T: 021 431 3855 F: 021 431 3496 E: orders@oaktreepress.com
W: www.oaktreepress.com